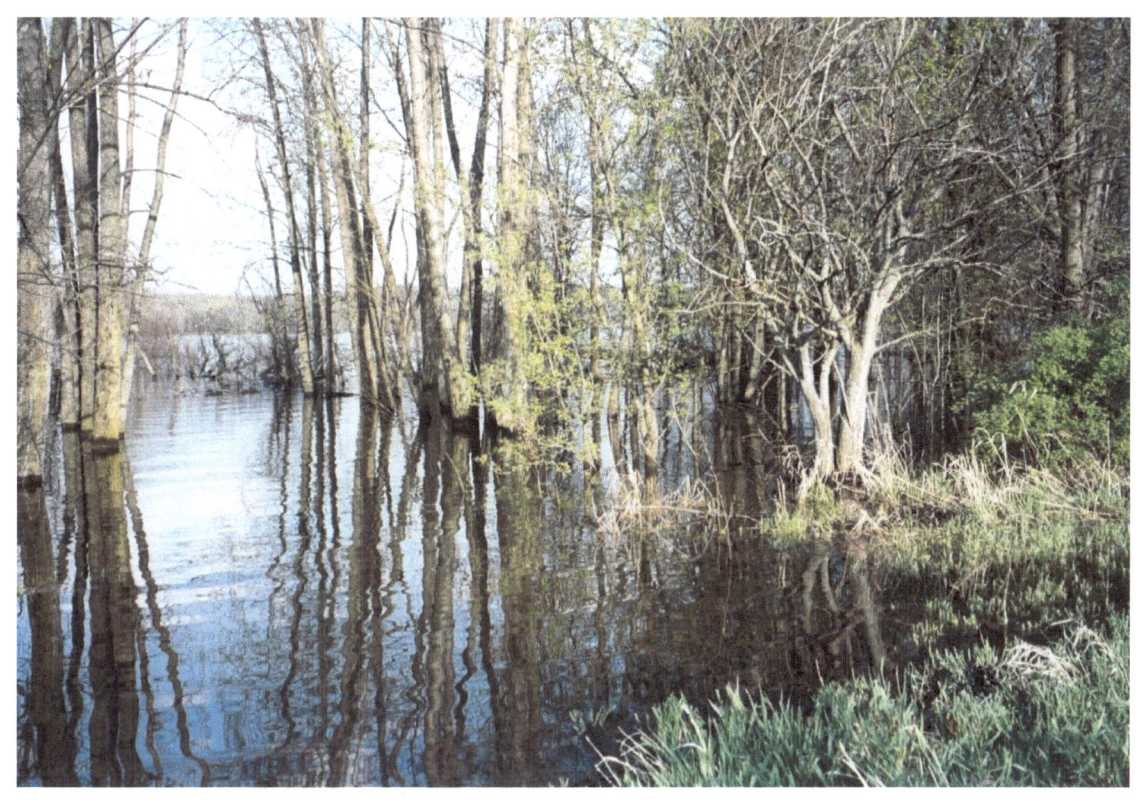

Reflections

Poetry, Photography, and Art

By Kelly L. Council

All Images & Poetry
Copyright © 2015-2020
By Kelly Council
All Rights Reserved

ISBN: 9798557719926

Published by KLiC Communications
www.kliccommunications.com
www.KellyCouncil.com

FOREWORD

"Some poets have a way of bringing us back into the middle of our own hearts. They pull us out from the clouds and bring us back into the reality of our own lives. We often forget these places or become too worldly to remember them. Kelly Council is such a poet. She makes me remember. She brings me back home. She touches my heart. These honest, passionate poems are full of love and depth. They reflect what poets feel and know and share. They make us young again."

Frank Theodore Kanelos
Poet Laureate of Birmingham, Alabama, 1996-1998

POETRY IN THIS BOOK HAS BEEN PREVIOUSLY PUBLISHED IN:

UAB's Aura Literary Arts Review (2013)

And other poetry books by the author:

Love and Excess Baggage (1994)
Footprints on My Heart (1998)
No Ordinary Moments (2000)
Flesh Still Missing (2002)

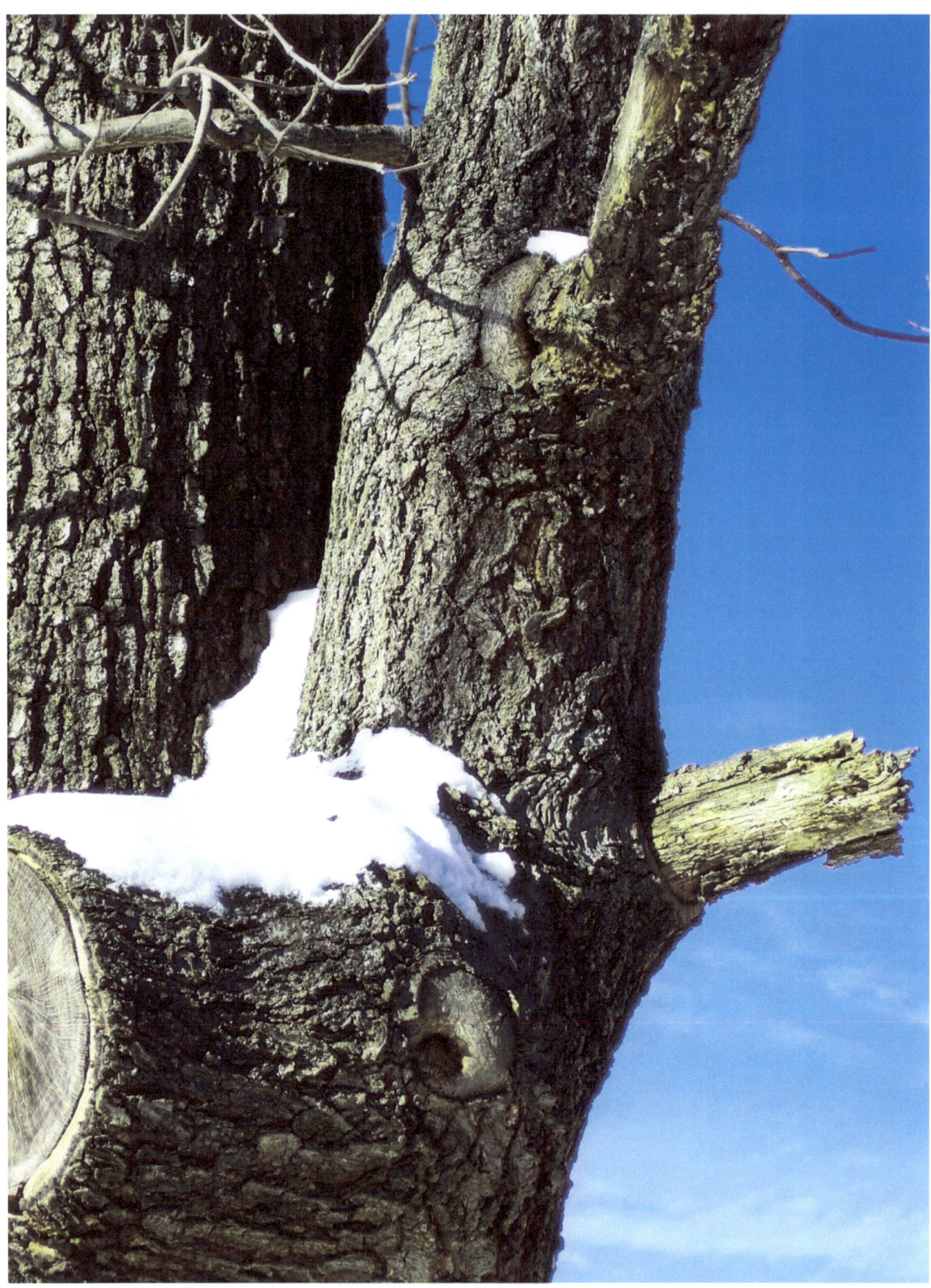

WINTER SOLSTICE

Perched on the edge,
In the last few days
Of the season,
The trees of fall
Hold on with might while

Strong autumn winds
Forcefully pull the
Last few colorful remnants
Of foliage from their limbs,
Leaving them bare.

Every year
This visual reminder
Of death
Forces much reflection
In my heart and soul.

This time finds me
Pondering life.
I want to be as
Naked as the trees
Surrendering fully,

As they do to the approaching solstice.
Exposed, they pass the days,
Bracing for the bitter chill,
All things right with the world
And as they should be.

As the cold sets in,
Their extremities become
More brittle with the exodus
Of each moment.
Still they stand, stunningly

In this most vulnerable state,
Ready to shoulder with absolute strength
And cradle with silent gentleness,
The weight of the
Impending snow.

When finally,
In the midst of winter,
In a perfect sense
Of utter brilliance,
Millions of tiny flakes

Descend from melancholy skies,
Some sticking softly
To subtlety paint
Myriad shades of brown
Sugar white.

Weaker boughs
Splinter and plunge beneath,
Under the cumulative
Force and burden
Of unwieldy ice shards.

With will and wisdom,
Frayed edges are released,
Preparing branches for new growth
And uncertain
Adventure,

Leaving twigs
And broken sticks
Amongst the dirt
That binds its roots
To Earth.

Blizzards, tornadoes,
Chaos and rain,
Precious memories of
A life weathered,
Offer their own invaluable rewards.

The process,
Necessary for the life cycle,
Prepares each precious temple
Of shade, shelter, serenity
For the rebirth of spring.

ANNIVERSARY

We must get through these days
And suffer alone,
Careful not to collapse
Under their heavy weight.
These loaded calendar days,
Which spark the soul's remembering.
These invisible cues
Of births, deaths,
Trials and tribulations,
The joys and laughter
Of our lives,
Anniversaries of what was,
But will never be again,
On these days, we must endure,
Quietly letting memories pass.

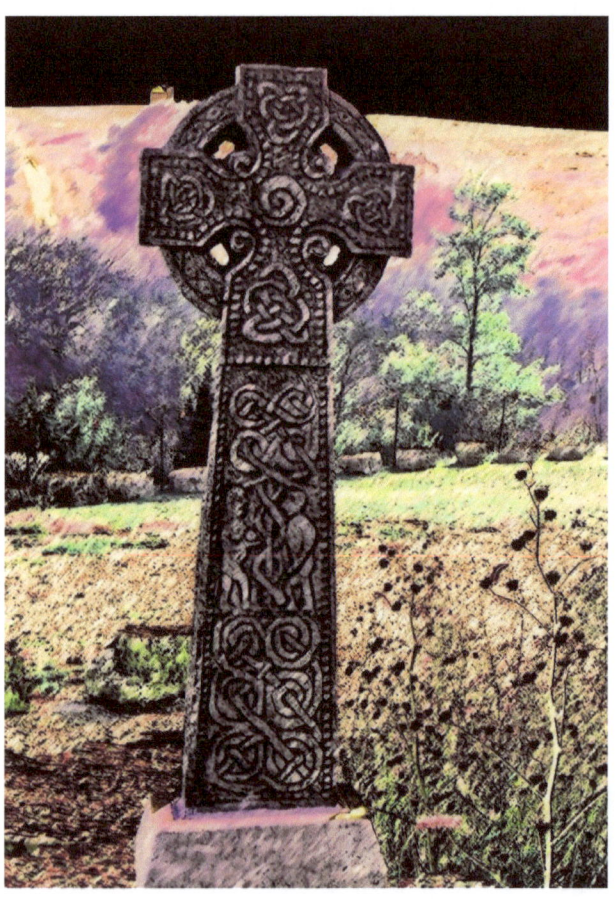

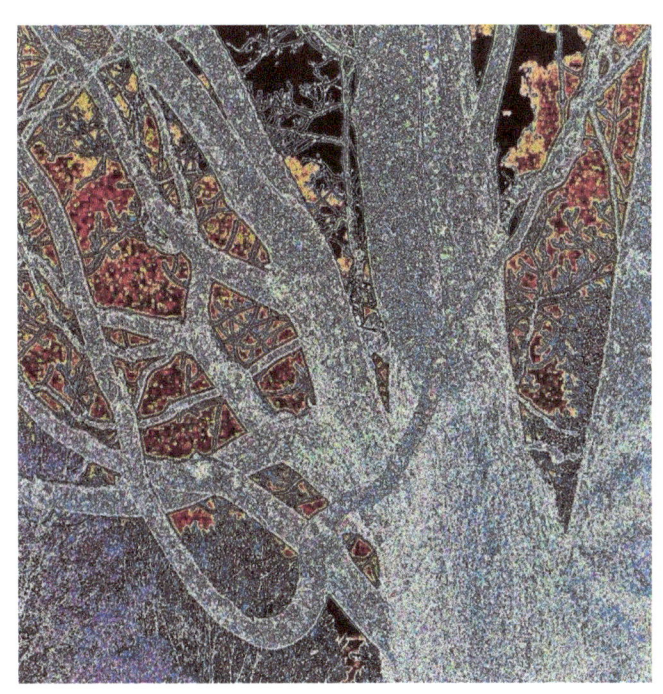

SYMPHONIC COLLAGE

I open my eyes, my ears, my heart.
I watch the leaves of Fall
Dance across the Earth,
Creating a mobile collage of color –
A feast for my sights,
Sounds vivid and unpredictable
Like the crackle of fire,
And loud like fingernails down a chalkboard,
When these discarded extremities meet pavement,
Creating a symphony for my ears.
This annual presentation –
Produced by the trees, directed by the wind –
Ignites my creative sensitivities,
Bringing a melancholy mood
Reminiscent of each Fall that fell before this one.
As my days grow shorter,
My memories grow longer
And heavier
And lighter
Through every passing year,
Recalling what went wrong,
What went right,
And what awaits the seasons ahead.

SELECTIVE MEMORY

Returning to that one-bedroom flat
Clouded your memory,
And in the shadows,
You saw only paradise.

You have forgotten
The storms
You had to weather
Within these walls.

Apparently, only I could hear
The secrets they whispered,
While you continued
To worship their shrill symphony,

Defacing the beautiful roses
You struggled so hard
To grow
In your own garden.

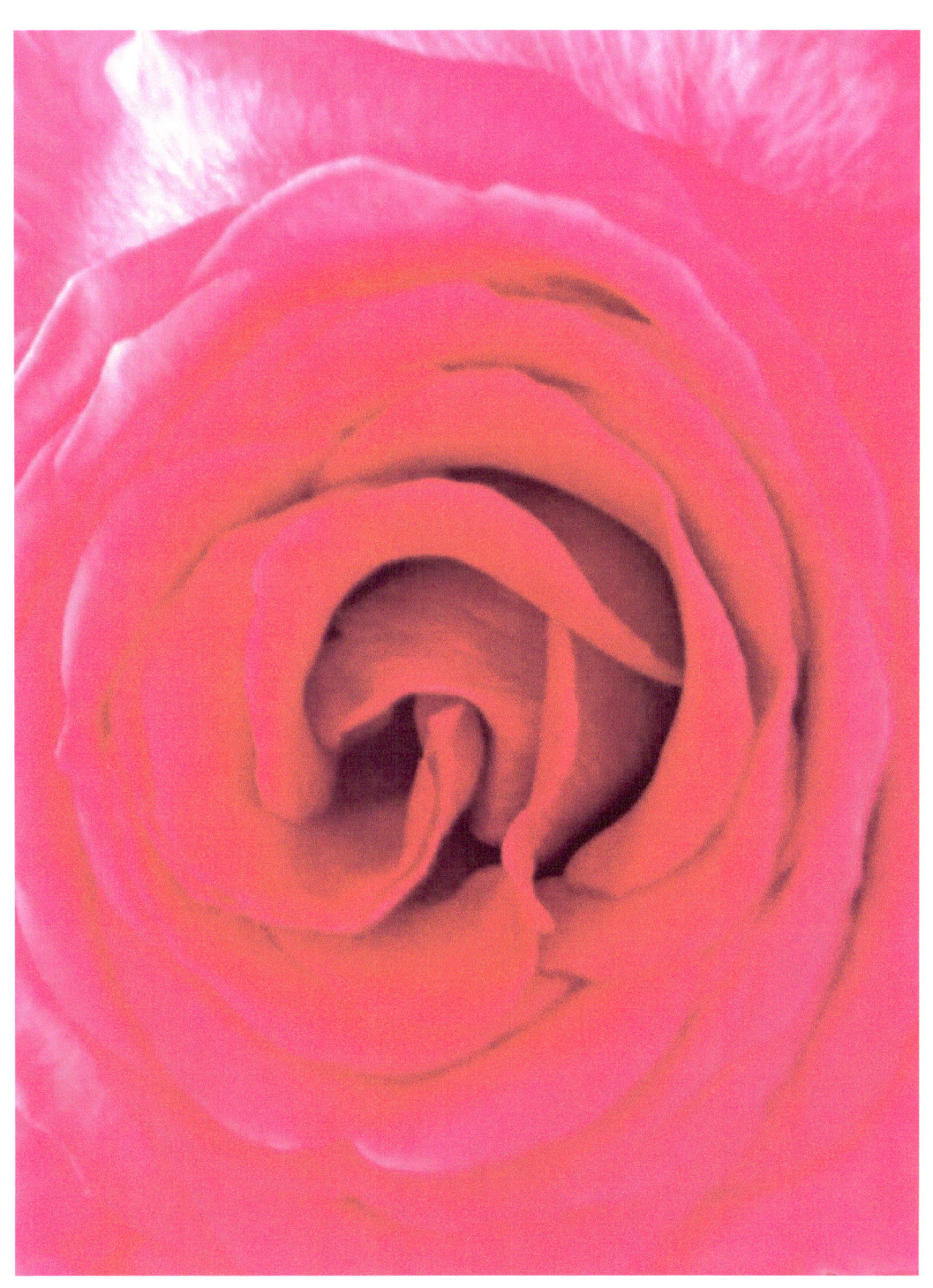

FOR THE LOVE OF A WOMAN
To All of Them, Each and Every One

There is something within her soul
I admire.
Could be the way
She lights her own fire.
She is spunky and chunky
With eyes that sparkle.
The things she says,
The things she does,
I think are remarkable.
She is beautiful, talented,
Spirited and free,
And most especially, I love the way
I see her in me.

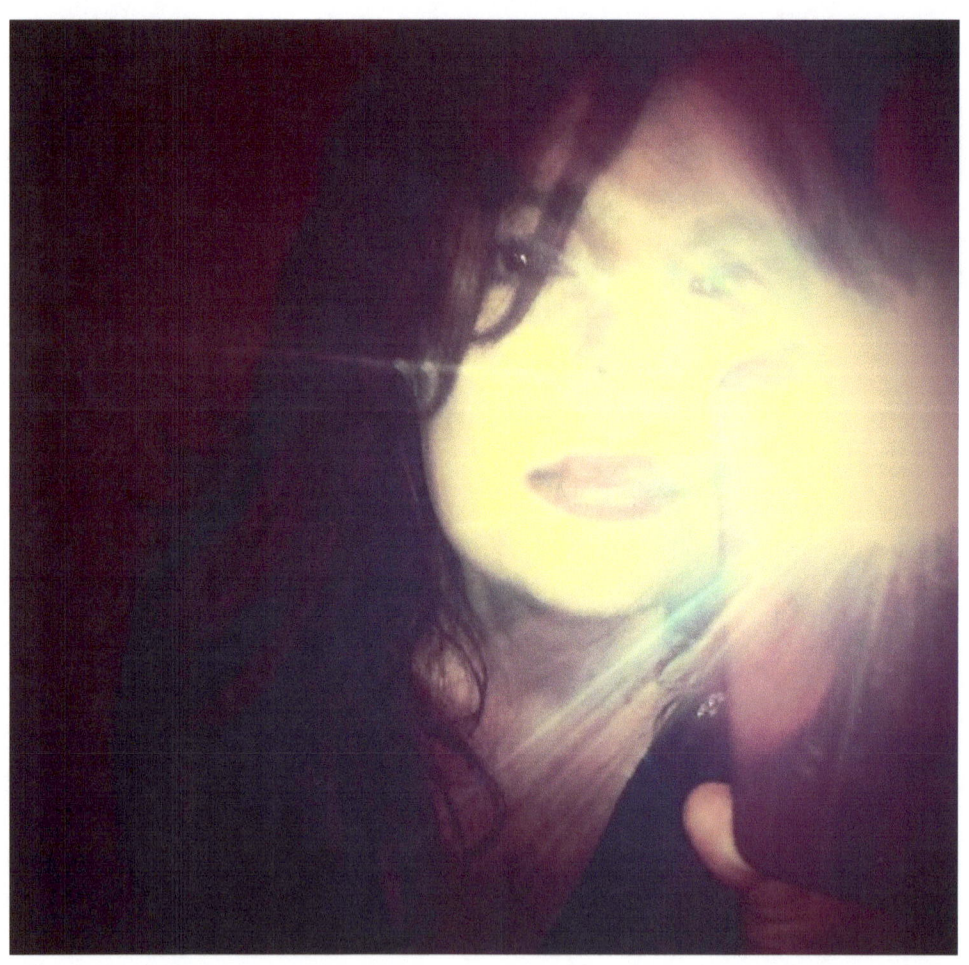

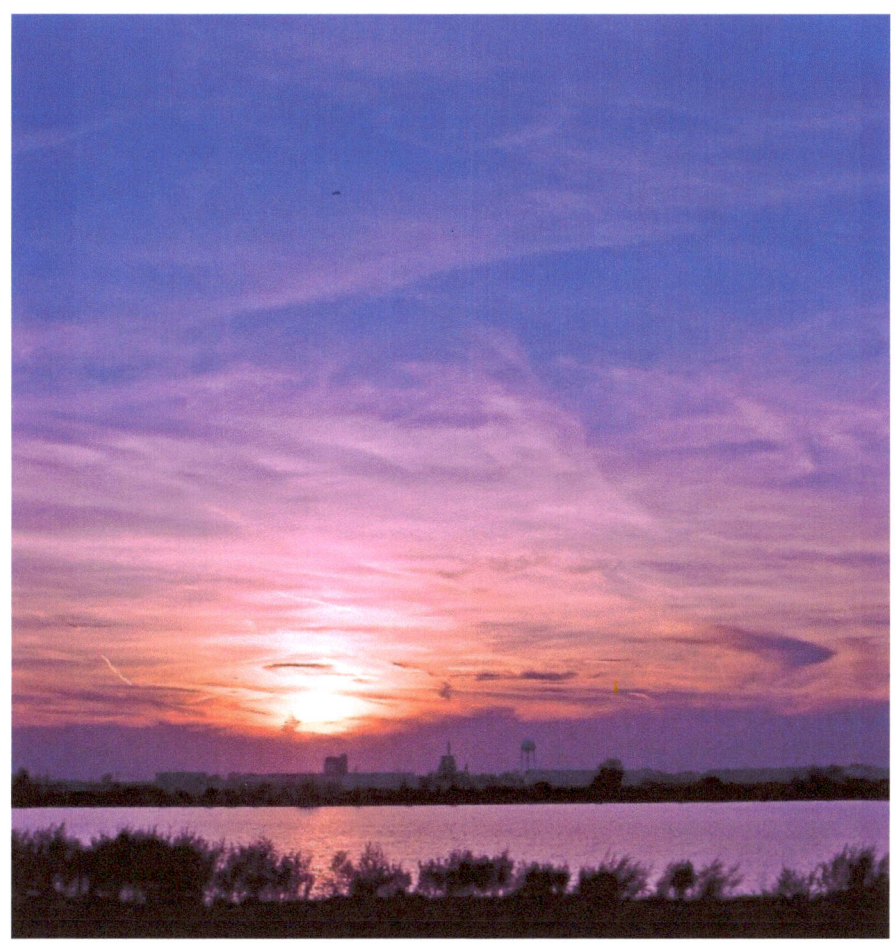

NO ORDINARY MOMENTS

So many friends' faces
Race through my mind's eye,
Speaking to the unforgettable marks
They have left upon my soul.
Their words of wisdom,
And acts of kindness,
Their spirits and histories,
Spill into my head,
Reminding me to treasure
Even the smallest interludes
Amid life's highs and lows,
Because there are
No ordinary moments.

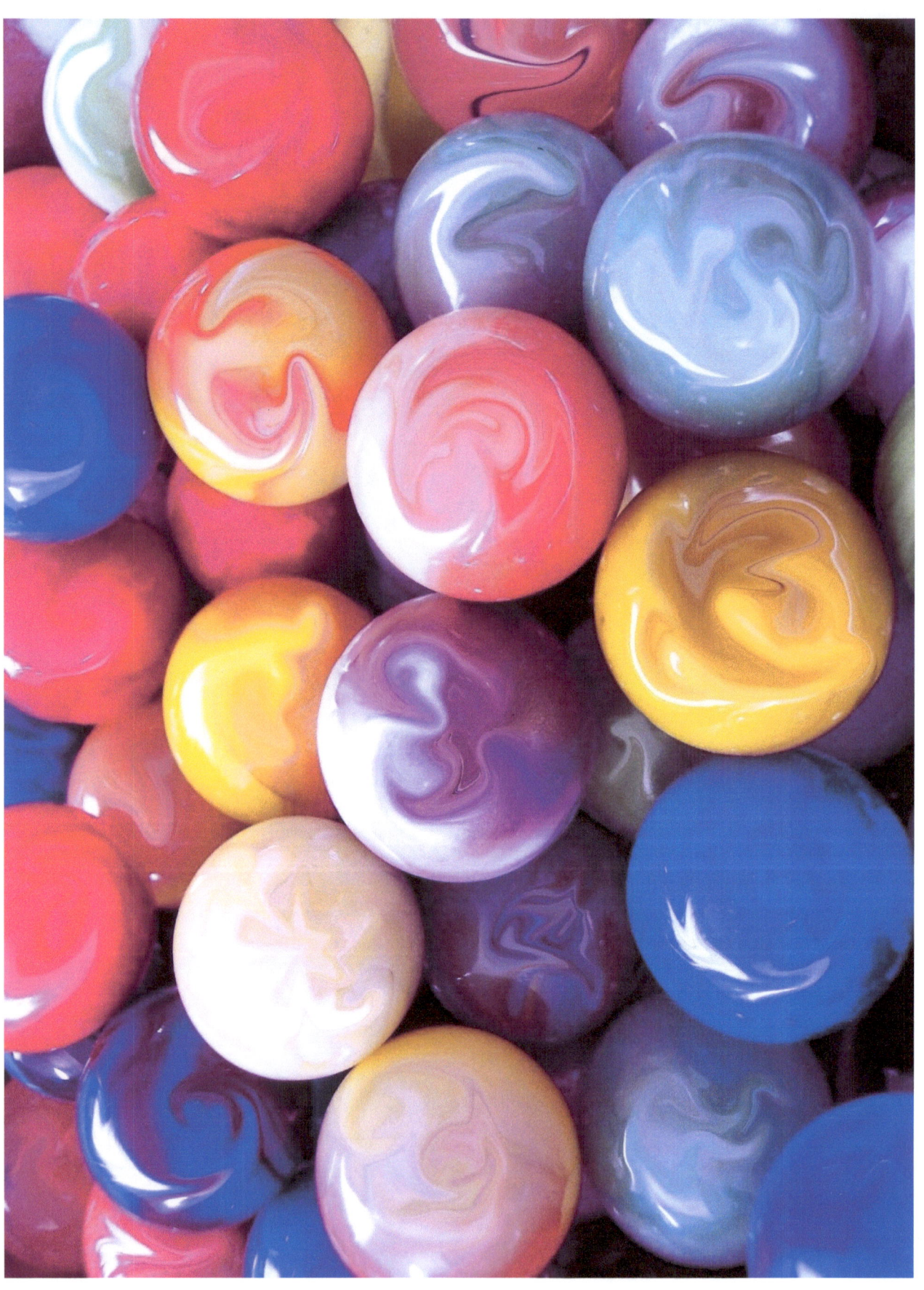

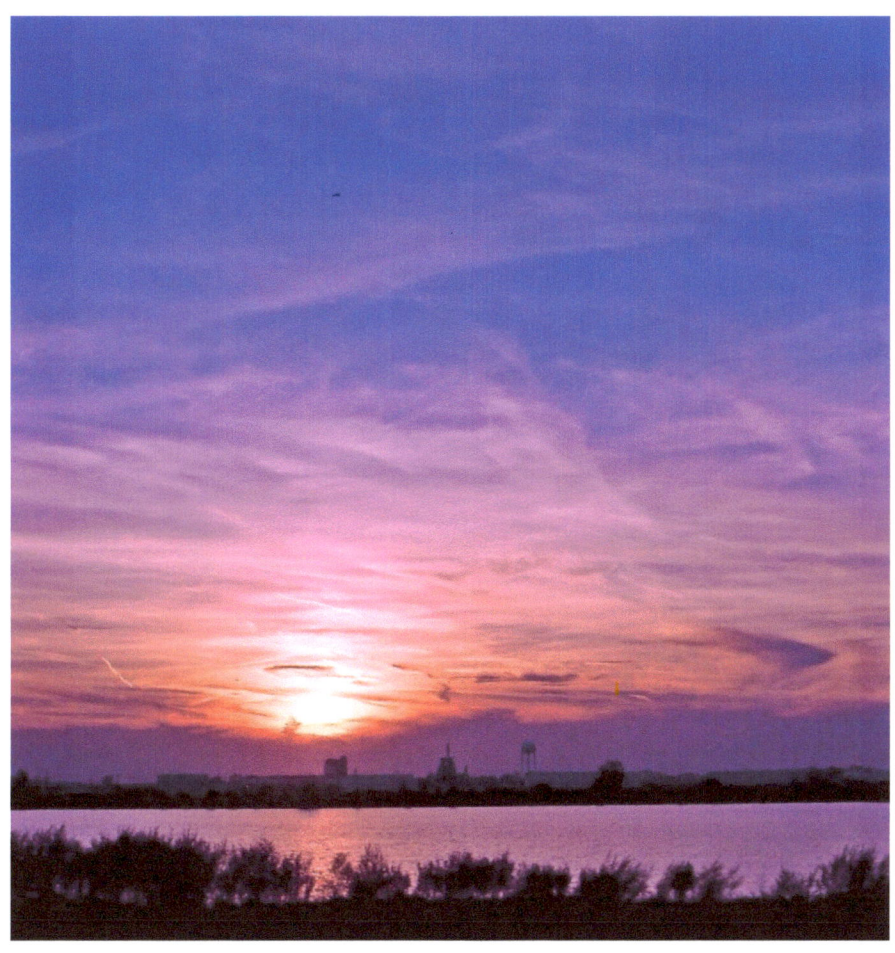

NO ORDINARY MOMENTS

So many friends' faces
Race through my mind's eye,
Speaking to the unforgettable marks
They have left upon my soul.
Their words of wisdom,
And acts of kindness,
Their spirits and histories,
Spill into my head,
Reminding me to treasure
Even the smallest interludes
Amid life's highs and lows,
Because there are
No ordinary moments.

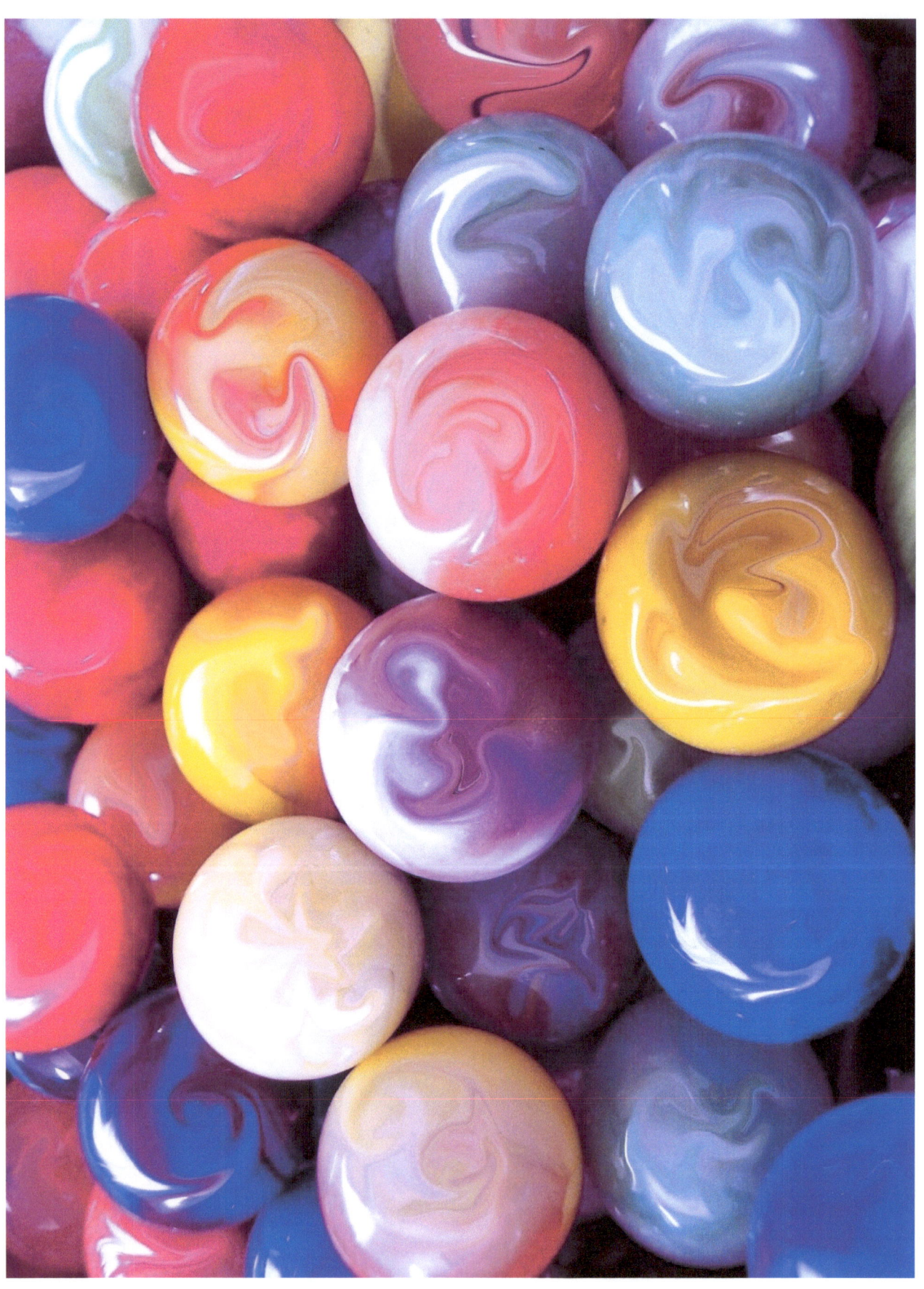

THE END

Revelation often leads
To new beginnings,
And sometimes
It is just an end
To hope
To love
To life
As we know it.

When you realize someone, some things
Are not as they seem,
An inevitable crack ensues,
Resulting in transformation.

We cannot return to what was.

The bridges we cross,
The bridges we burn,
The bridges we mend,

There is an order to life
That we all must follow.
But some of us don't.
Some of us won't.

DAYS LOST

Lately, I have been seeing signs of
Destiny everywhere,
Signs of the word,
Not of my own.
That is always
Harder to find,
Like searching in a haystack
For the years of life
That have passed us by.
How many days
Have you lost
Wondering what
You are missing?

STREETLIGHT

A solitary streetlight
Illuminates my darkened room
Through paned windows,
Guiding my passage
To the world beyond.
As I drift
Into slumber,
I dream of visions
Beyond my wakeful state.

ONLY HUMAN

I put my pen to paper,
Eloquent words flow through,
But never enough.
I struggle to close
The gaps
Between barriers,
To relate to
The human experience.

WRITER'S BLOCK

The words of my heart
Never come
When I need them.
They tease me,
Wanting and waiting,
They finally pour
With a precise timing
Beyond my wisdom.

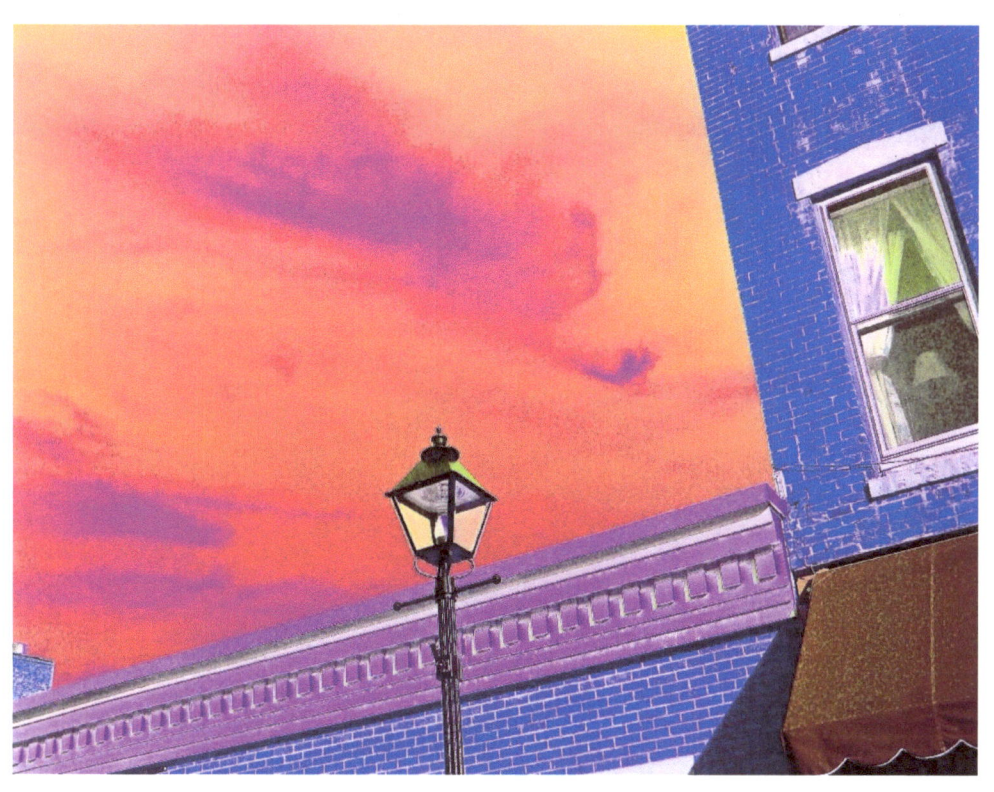
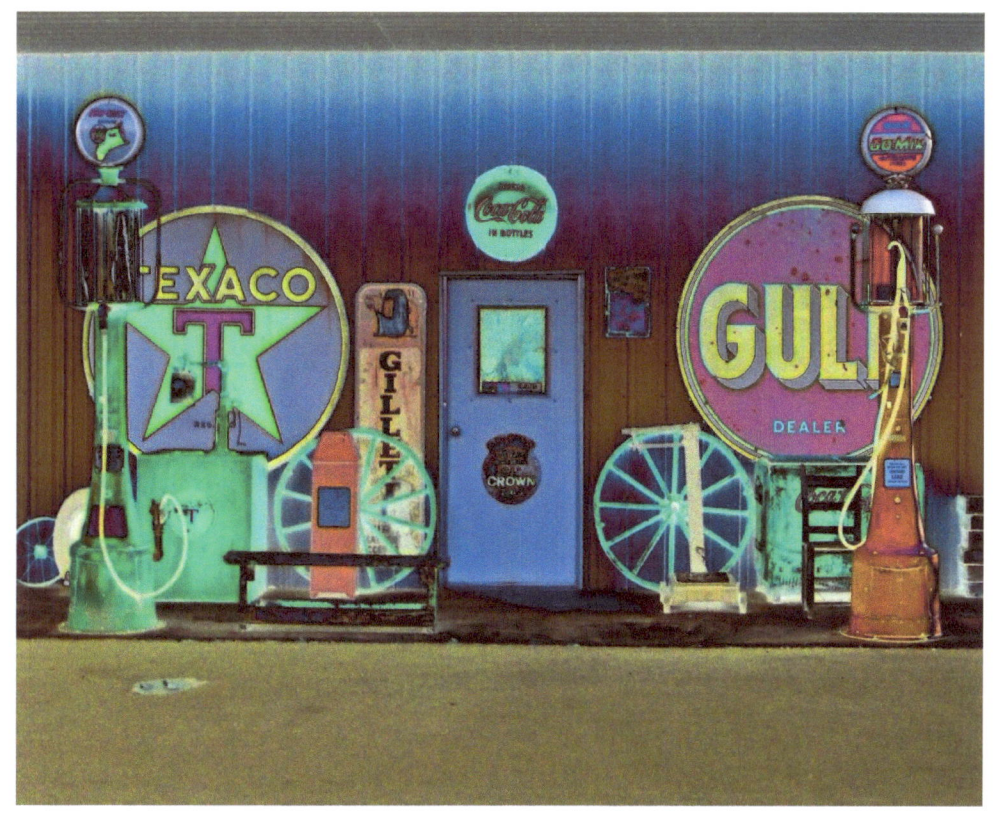

LIFE ELEMENTS

Air/wood/water/earth/fire
Sky/trees/oceans/lands/sun,
A collage of color
On this late fall afternoon
Offers an ever-present,
Constantly-altering reminder
Of peace,
Stilling me
In my own times of transformation.
I am grateful for these elements,
Always changing,
Always the same,
No matter where I travel.

FREE FLIGHT

Neither the sea
Nor the winds
Could move me
As much as your eyes
The day I first soared
With you.

Neither the Earth
Nor the sea
Nor the wind
Could set me free
As much as your love
For me.

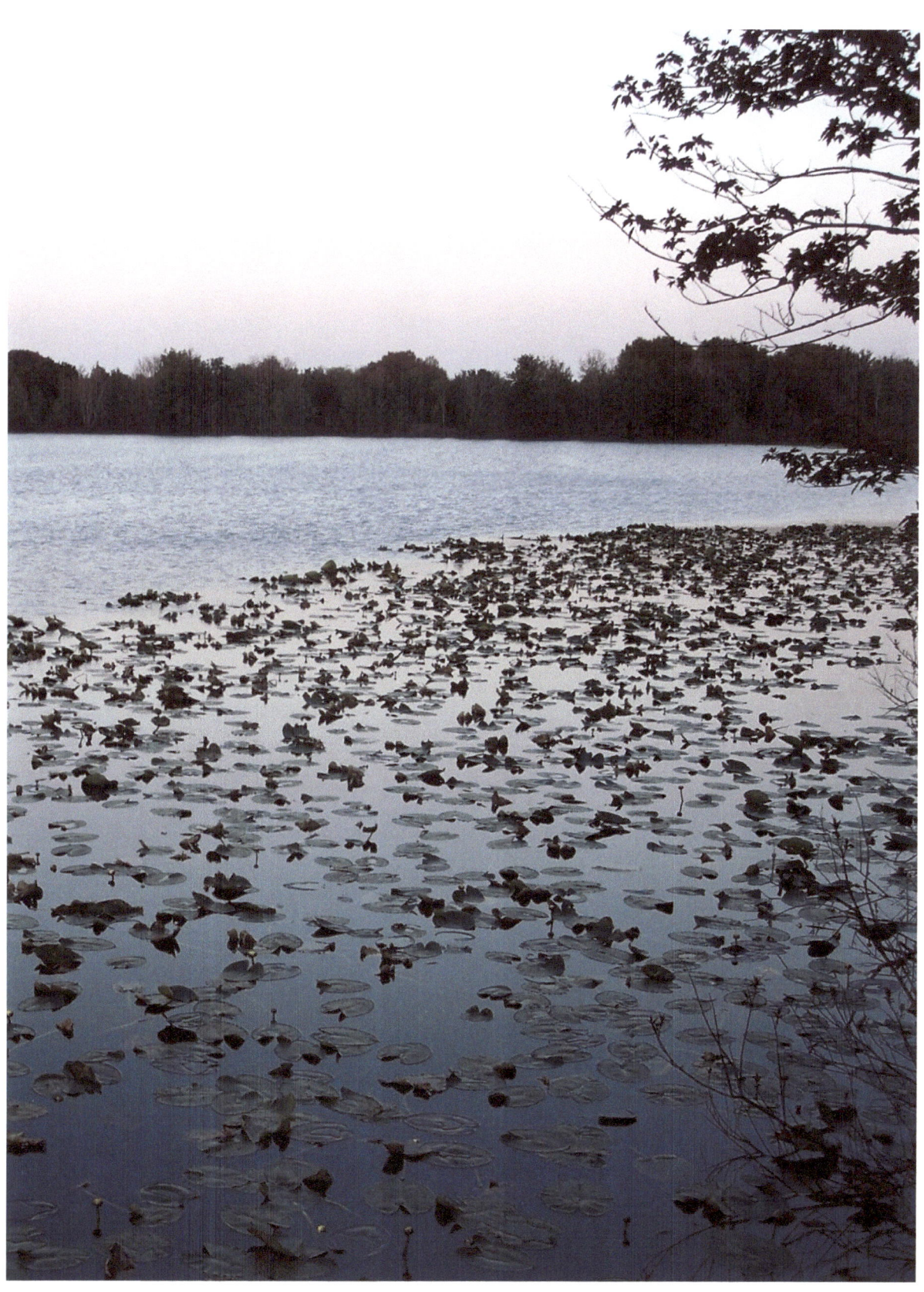

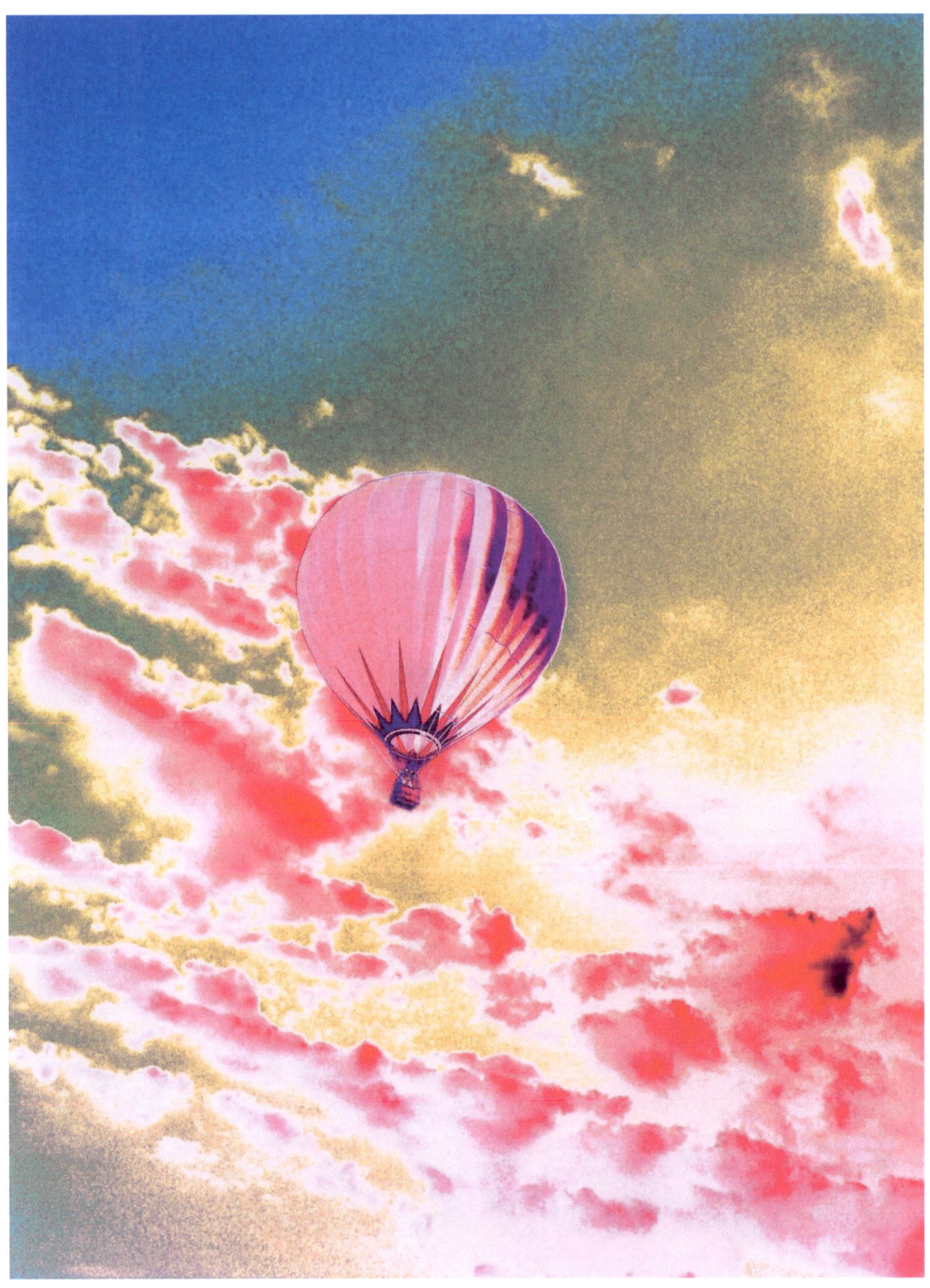

PEACE

I feel most at peace
When I am high
On all that is
This life
And all the joy
It can hold.
The more I am grateful,
The more I have to be grateful for.
The more I love,
The more I have to love.
The more I live,
The more alive and
At peace I feel.
It is through this peace that I grow
Into whom I want to be,
Into the woman I am to be,
Into who
I am.

SATURDAY MORNINGS

Saturday mornings
I used to wake
To the sound of your voice
Beckoning me to come
Crawl into bed with you
And watch "The Pink Panther."
How I used to love
To climb into the safety
Of your arms and
Rest my head
On your chest and shoulders.
Sometimes,
We would get into tickle fights
During commercial breaks
And before the aroma
Of bacon, eggs, and grits
Summoned us to breakfast.
Now on Saturday mornings,
I just sleep late
Since you and the Panther
Have been gone for years.

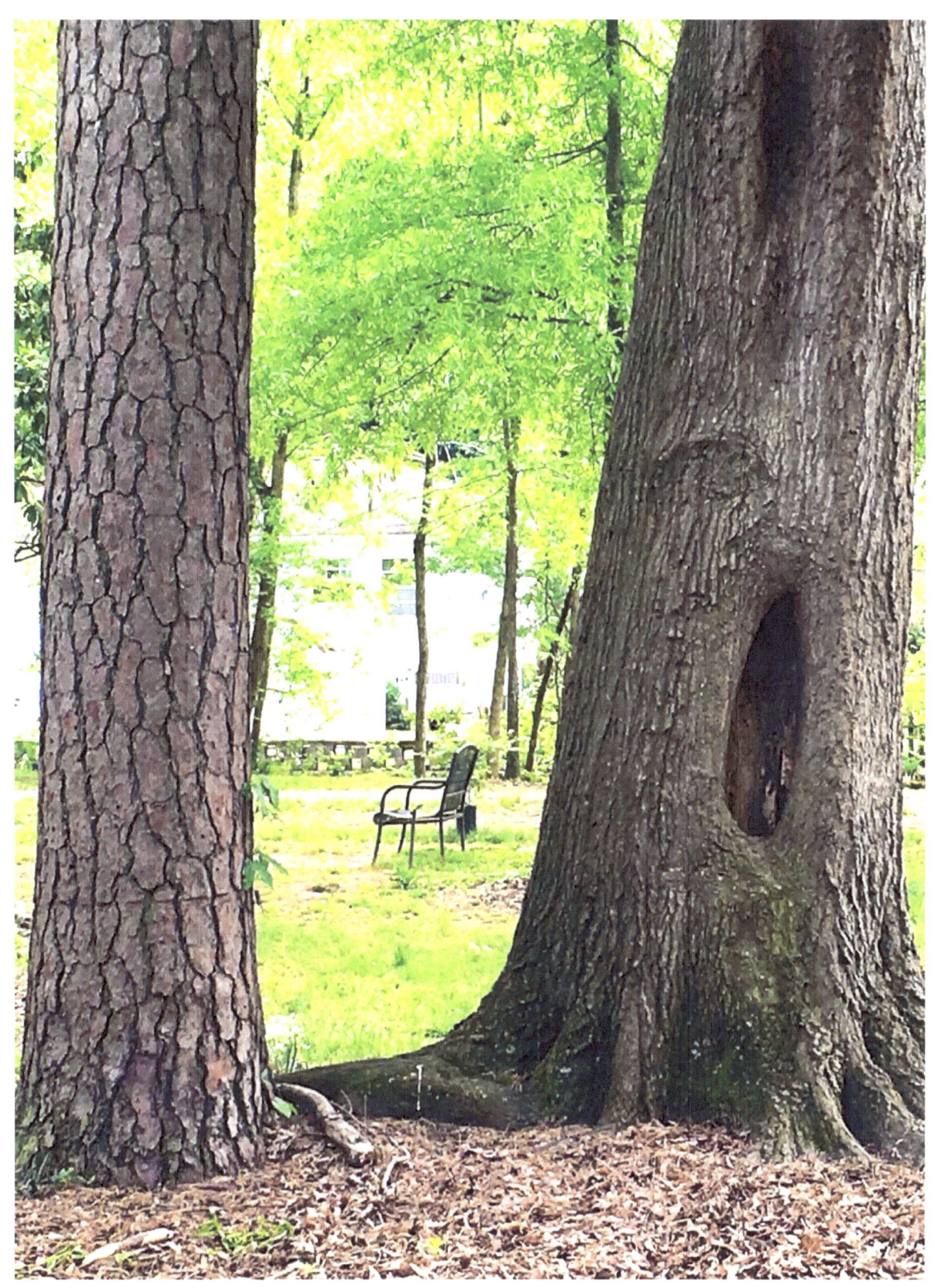

ABOUT THE AUTHOR

Born in 1968 in Birmingham, Alabama, Kelly Council holds a Bachelor of Arts in Communication and Journalism from the University of Alabama at Birmingham. She is an Internationally-collected poet, photographer, and artist who loves spending time with her beloved family and friends, and traveling wherever life takes her. In addition to living for many years in Alabama, she has resided in Ohio, Indiana, Florida, Kentucky, Missouri, and Texas. Her professional experience includes working in the fields of writing, reporting, editing, marketing, market research, public relations, teaching, management, fund raising, sales, network marketing, consulting, and administration, sometimes all while holding the same position. She currently owns and operates her own social media and marketing agency and an ecommerce business. She also travels throughout the United States and abroad whenever an adventure is available. Her mission is to enrich the lives of others by fostering serenity in our stressful world and to help people recognize their own phenomenal talents, gifts, potential, and possibilities. This is Kelly's fifth book of poetry. To learn more, visit kliccommunications.com. Photography prints available at kellycouncil.com.

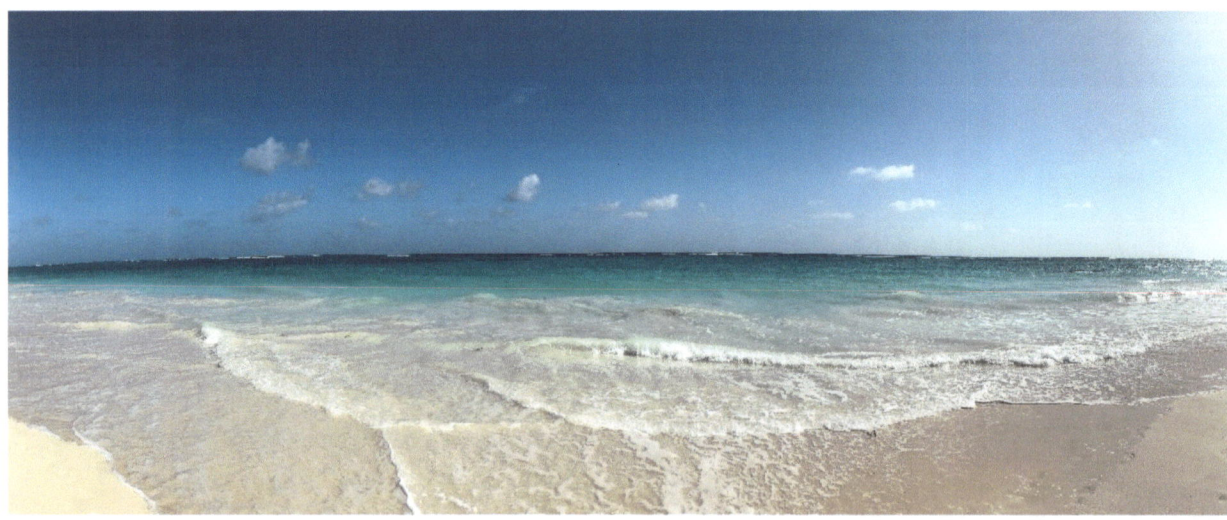

www.ingramcontent.com/pod-product-compliance
Lightning Source LLC
Chambersburg PA
CBHW051838210526
45473CB00005B/1924